STRANGE BUT TRUE

22 Amazing Stories

by DONALD J. SOBOL

D1018321

SCHOLASTIC INC.
New York Toronto London Auckland Sydney

For
Larry and Tommy

0-590-42431-9

12 11 10   4 5 6 7 8 9/9 0/0

Printed in the U.S.A.   01

Contents

Author's Note

Of the twenty-two stories in this book, nineteen are based on easily found facts. The other three tell about ghosts: "Girl on the Train," "The Elevator Operator," and "Rex."

Ghosts and reports of ghosts are not easy to check. Without objective clues, ghost hunters must depend on the word of the viewer. Did he or she really see something? Who can say?

What we can say is this: In each of the ghost stories included here a person *thought* he saw something very strange. And each of the viewers was convinced that what he saw was an actual ghost. These people honestly felt they were reporting what was true. That is why these ghost stories have been included in a book called *Strange but True*.

But remember, as you read them, that we have only the word of the viewers. *No one has yet proved that ghosts walk among us.*

—D. S.

He Carried a Curse

His first name was Robert, and he might have been President of the United States had he chosen to run for the office.

Instead he served his country ably in subordinate roles — as secretary of war under two Presidents and as minister to Great Britain under a third.

In private life he was a successful lawyer and became head of the Pullman Company. Yet he came to believe that he carried a special curse.

As a youthful captain in the Army, he stood beside the bed of President Lincoln only hours after Lincoln had been shot. The President died.

As secretary of war, he hurried to the railroad station in Washington, D.C., to tell President Garfield he could not accompany him to Elberon, New Jersey. He arrived to find the President had just been shot. The President died.

As a leading businessman, he was invited by President McKinley to meet him at the Pan American Exposition in Buffalo, New York. When he arrived, he learned that the President had just been shot. The President died.

From that day forward, Robert never allowed himself near a President. He declined all invitations to the White House.

"If they only knew," he remarked in private, "they wouldn't want me."

Once, upon being asked if he would be at an event where a President was to appear, he reportedly said, "No, I am not going, and they'd better not invite me. There is a certain fatality about Presidential functions when I am present."

The man who believed that somehow he had been the instrument of death to three martyred Presidents was laid to rest forever in 1926—61 years after the assassination of his father, Abraham Lincoln.

The Floating Coffin

On the morning of August 12, 1775, the Greenland whaleship *Herald* was picking her way among the icebergs of the North Atlantic. Suddenly the lookout bellowed.

"A ship! A ship . . . west ahead!"

On deck, the *Herald*'s captain turned in surprise. Some three miles away he saw masts poking above an iceberg. Slowly, a three-masted schooner drifted into view.

Her sails hung in tatters. Ice coated her spars and rigging. She glistened in the sun. Captain Warren studied her through his telescope. He saw no signs of life.

Veering close, he hailed the strange ship. Silence greeted his shouts. The schooner continued on her seemingly aimless way.

"Lower the longboat," Captain Warren ordered. "I'm going to have a look."

His crew were superstitious and had no mind to venture aboard a ghostly ship. Never theless, they obeyed. Captain Warren picked eight men and rowed over.

As the longboat neared the schooner's stern, the men made out her name — *Octavius*. She was unknown to them.

Again Captain Warren hailed her. Only rotting timbers and the wind in the loose rigging answered him, creaking and whispering.

With four of his crew, the captain climbed aboard. The deck was slippery with ice and crusted snow. Seeing no one topside, the boarding party went below.

In the crew's quarters they found twenty-eight men, frozen to death. Each lay in his bunk heavily bundled in blankets and clothing. The fierce Arctic cold had perfectly preserved their bodies.

Next the investigating crew entered the cabin of the captain, whose body was seated in a chair by a worktable.

In a cabin behind this one, were three more corpses.

A woman lay in one bunk, her head resting lifelike on her elbow. The body of a man sat cross-legged on the floor in one corner. His hands held a flint and a piece of steel. Before him was a pile of woodshavings. Death had overtaken him as he had struggled to light a fire.

Alongside the man was a sailor's jacket.

Captain Warren lifted it. Beneath was the body of a small boy.

The men of the *Herald* had seen enough. They wanted to get off at once.

But the captain wanted to investigate further. He managed to inspect a galley, but he found no food there. By then his men were on the verge of panic and threatening mutiny.

Taking the schooner's logbook, Captain Warren reluctantly returned to his ship. He watched the *Octavius* and her cargo of death drift northward out of sight. She would never be seen again.

Later, when he retired to his cabin to read the logbook, the captain discovered that all but the first and last pages were missing. The sailor to whom he had entrusted the book had allowed the rest to fall out.

The first page included the information that *Octavius* had departed England, bound for the China trade, on September 10, 1761 — *fourteen years earlier!*

The last page had but a single entry. It was dated November 11, 1762, and read: "We have now been enclosed in ice seventeen days. Our approximate position is Longitude 160 W, Latitude 75 N. The fire went out yesterday and our master has been trying to rekindle it, but without success. He has handed the steel and flint to the mate. The master's son died this morning and his wife says she no longer feels the terrible cold. The rest of us have no relief from the agony."

Captain Warren's eyes returned to the words "Longitude 160 W, Latitude 75 N . . ." The meaning was incredible . . .

On the day of the last entry in the logbook, *Octavius* had been icebound in the Arctic Ocean north of Point Barrow, Alaska — thousands of miles from where Captain Warren had just boarded her! A continent of ice lay between these two points.

What *Octavius* had negotiated was the legendary Northwest Passage. For hundreds of years sea captains had sought a shorter route between the Atlantic and the Pacific to carry trade between Europe and the Far East. The Northwest Passage was a dream that could eliminate the long voyage around the tip of South America.

Apparently the captain of the *Octavius* also had decided to try to find the Northwest Passage, instead of sailing home to England around South America. He had tried, and like so many before, he had found death instead.

But the *Octavius* had succeeded on her own. Year after year she had sailed on, her ship's wheel unattended. She had inched eastward through the vast fields of ice, blindly withstanding the fury of the elements till she finally floated again in the North Atlantic.

Not until 1906 — one hundred and thirty years later — did another ship, *Gjoa*, commanded by the Norwegian explorer Roald Amundsen, navigate the Northwest Passage.

But *Octavius* had been first — carrying a captain and crew who had been frozen for thirteen years!

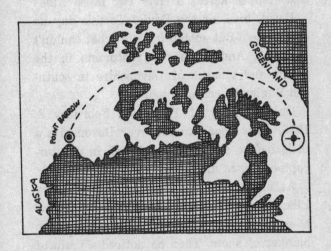

The Night Thing

What was it that walked through stone walls, jumped over eighteen-foot haystacks, and stepped across a river two miles wide?

Beast, bird, or the Devil? To this day no one knows. But *something* did what couldn't be done. And it left its footprints in the towns and villages of Devonshire in southern England a century ago.

On the night of Thursday, February 8, 1885, snow began to fall over Devonshire a little before eight o'clock. It fell in uninterrupted silence until nearly midnight.

At six o'clock the next morning, Henry Pilk, a baker in Topsham, stepped from his house. He paused briefly to admire the blanket of snow. Then he noticed a train of footprints across his enclosed yard.

Each print was U-shaped, as if made by the shoe of a pony or donkey.

Henry Pilk frowned. The footprints, or

hoofprints, were all in a line — one in front of the other. No man or animal walked like that, as if on a tightrope.

Henry Pilk was not a curious fellow. He shrugged, went into his bakehouse, and started his day's labors.

An hour later the whole town was abuzz. Others had discovered the hoofprints. Eagerly they sought to catch a glimpse of the creature responsible.

At the start it was all great fun. But the longer the trackers followed the single line of prints, the stronger grew their sense of uneasiness.

Whatever had visited them during the night possessed extraordinary powers. In places the hoofprints led right up to garden walls of stone as high as twelve feet. The prints stopped at the base — and resumed on the other side as though no wall stood in the way!

Could the creature have jumped over? Hardly. The depth of the prints in the snow never changed. Neither did their size, which measured four inches by two and a half inches. And without exception, they were spaced eight inches apart.

Moreover, the trail never doubled back though it led up to every house in town. Why? Was the creature marking the occupants?

While the people of Topsham puzzled nervously, the mystery spread and deepened. As far south as Totnes, the same single trail had been seen in dozens of places.

The distance between Topsham and Totnes is about ninety-six miles on a straight line. The snowstorm had ended at midnight. Six hours later Henry Pilk discovered the tracks. In six hours, what could have moved fast enough on a wandering, zigzag course to reach points ninety-six miles apart?

Nothing known in that day or unearthed in this.

Prints were found in cemeteries, atop wagons, on beaches and roofs, in woods and marketplaces, and up to — and beyond — eighteen-foot-high haystacks.

Prints were tracked to the edge of the Exe River where it was two miles wide, and picked up again on the opposite bank. A similar crossing was found a few miles to the south.

Everywhere the horseshoe prints were the same; four inches by two and a half inches, at intervals of eight inches. Nowhere in the snow was there a sign that the creature had rested.

Fun and curiosity gave way to uneasiness. Presently superstition and fear took command.

As the snow melted, the tracks blurred. The prints began to resemble a cloven hoof. Who but the Devil had a cloven hoof? Who but the Devil would peer into the dwellings of God-fearing folk and mark the sinners?

Women and children hid in their homes behind barred doors and shutters. The men fetched their dogs. Armed with muskets, pistols, clubs, and pitchforks, they grimly tramped the countryside. Apparently nobody paused to consider how to capture the Devil once he was cornered.

That difficulty never arose. The night prowler — beast, phantom, or Devil — passed unseen. Plenty of snow fell in the days that followed, but the tracks never reappeared.

For weeks afterward, men went about carrying weapons, and lonely trails were avoided. Clergymen preached about "the signs in our midst" as warnings from heaven about drinking, swearing, and loose living.

The *London Times* and other newspapers carried many columns about the strange hoofprints. Expert opinion abounded like wild berries.

The prints, it was claimed, were made by giant leaping rats, huge rabbits, birds, otters, toads, kangaroos. Richard Owen, a respected naturalist, blamed the badger without ever having seen the prints.

None of the explanations fitted the facts: thousands of hoofprints in a single line; exactly four inches by two and a half inches; exactly eight inches apart; roaming tirelessly, in absolute silence, at uncanny speed over and through every obstacle.

The men and women who struggled with the mystery are gone. But the questions linger . . .

Where had the night thing come from? Where was it going?

And when would it walk again?

Girl on the Train

Awakening from his nap, the American painter Girard Hale saw a girl seated opposite him. When he had dozed off, he had been alone in the compartment of the speeding French train.

Hale was more pleased than surprised by his companion. She was lovely, and yet her face was fixed in brooding sadness. The artist was charmed.

He struck up a conversation. To his delight, the girl quickly turned to the subject of painting. Although they had never met, she knew quite a bit about his work.

Suddenly she asked an odd question. Could he paint from memory the portrait of a person he had seen only once?

"For example, could you paint me from memory?" she asked, sitting down beside him.

"Yes," replied Hale with conviction. "But I'd rather paint you from life."

The train slowed to a halt. The girl got off.

"We shall meet once more," she said in parting.

Hale's stop was ten miles farther on. He had been working in Paris when he had been commissioned to do a portrait of a French woman at her home on the Loire River. It was 1928.

Upon reaching his destination, Hale was graciously received. He changed his clothes and made his way downstairs for dinner. In the hall he encountered the girl with whom he'd spoken on the train.

She greeted him with a brilliant smile. "I promised we should meet once more," she said.

Hale marveled at how quickly she had arrived at the house. "Tell me how you did it," he said, laughing. "I should like to travel the same way."

For a fleeting moment the smile slipped from the girl's lips. "That would be impossible," she said softly and hurried away.

During dinner with his host and his hostess — the woman whose portrait he had been commissioned to paint — Hale offhandedly remarked about the girl.

His host stiffened. "I have no idea whom you met," he said forcefully. "There is no young woman in this house. My wife and I are not expecting one."

Seeing his host's peculiar reaction, Hale switched the talk to other things. But the topic was reopened at the coffee table. Hale was asked to make a sketch of the girl's face, and was supplied with pencil and paper.

Hale settled himself and began to draw. The pencil seemed to guide his hand as it reproduced an exact likeness of the girl.

He was putting the finishing touches to the sketch when his hostess fainted and slipped from her chair to the floor.

After she had been revived, her husband stared gravely at the drawing.

"It is our daughter whom you met on the train and in the hall," he said somberly to Hale. "The sketch you made from memory can be of no one else."

He picked up the paper and carefully tore it into pieces.

"She died many years ago."

The Clue in the Sand

One of the strangest of all detective cases took place on a beach in France in 1888.

It began the day a businessman named André Monet and his wife arrived at the small French seaside town of St. Adresse for a vacation. Late that night, Monet left his hotel to take a swim before going to bed.

He never returned.

Early the next morning a boy discovered him lying on the beach, dead of a bullet wound.

The French national police sent Detective Robert Le Dru to investigate. Oddly, Le Dru happened to be in Le Havre, which was within walking distance of St. Adresse.

Le Dru was selected to go to the scene of the crime because of his reputation, not because he chanced to be nearby. He was considered brilliant. Not only was he the youngest detective on the police force, he was easily the most successful at solving mysteries.

It was claimed that he could sniff a used but empty glass and identify the drink, and could look at a footprint and describe the person who made it. His superiors believed him a wizard at swiftly finding and reading clues.

The truth was something else. Robert Le Dru was neither swift nor brilliant. He was patient and thorough. Far from solving mysteries at a glance, he worked slowly and carefully.

He spent hours and even days at the scene of a crime, going over every foot of ground. He scarcely slept until he had checked out every clue, every alibi, every suspect. By dogged determination, he had built a dazzling record.

That record was his lifeblood, and he did everything to further it. For example, he never admitted that he had toiled around the clock tracing the owner of a button. In his report, he wrote only that he had deduced who the owner was.

To his superiors he seemed the ideal man to send to the beach at St. Adresse. And he was. No one but Robert Le Dru could have solved the murder of André Monet.

But when the great detective arrived at St.

Adresse, he could uncover no leads. The murdered man had no known enemies. He had not been robbed. His only heir was his wife, and she had waited up for him in the hotel lobby in view of the night clerk until 2:30 A.M. Since the coroner had fixed the time of death at no later than 2 A.M., she was cleared.

Le Dru was making no progress. Worse, the many nights during which he had passed up sleep in order to work on his cases were catching up with him. He was exhausted and his nerves were strung taut. Oh, how he longed for time to rest! How he would sleep — peaceful sleep! He had told no one about his nightmares . . .

Before he could rest, however, there was this new murder to solve. Night fell, and still his efforts led him no closer to the killer.

He resorted to his tried and tested tools — patience and painstaking thoroughness. He marked a large circle around the spot where the body had lain. Lantern in hand, he examined every inch of sand, in and near the circle.

Near midnight he found the clue, a footprint. It told him the identity of the murderer, and it shook him to the bone. For the footprint was what he had been half-consciously looking for all along — and dreaded to find. The guilty man was someone he had known all his life.

The struggle within Le Dru was soul-wrenching. Should he turn the murderer in? Duty at last overcame every personal objection. After walking the beach for hours, Robert Le Dru entered the St. Adresse police station.

He had solved the case, he announced, and laid upon the desk a plaster cast of a footprint. It was of the left foot.

The footprint unquestionably belonged to the murderer, the detective asserted. He had sneaked up behind his victim in stocking feet.

As proof, Le Dru pointed to the plaster cast. The first joint of the big toe was missing.

Then he stooped and took off his own shoe.

"Gentlemen," he said quietly, "I am the murderer."

He had lost the first joint of the big toe on his left foot while a boy. The nightmares, in which he saw himself commit murder, had come true!

Le Dru was placed under arrest and eventually brought to trial. Respected doctors testified in his defense. Due to a rare mental condition, they stated, Robert Le Dru was dangerous only at night. During the day, he was perfectly sane.

The words of the doctors, plus a masterly plea by his lawyer, saved Le Dru from execution. He was sentenced to life imprisonment.

The sentence was carried out only in the hours between sunset and sunrise. During the daylight, he was set free to go wherever he chose.

Robert Le Dru died in his cell in 1939. For fifty-one years he served his unique sentence, walking the streets during the day and returning at night to be locked up.

The Holdout

The two men crouched, listening. Since sundown they had been hunting in the jungles of Guam, one of the Marianas islands in the Pacific, where Americans and Japanese had fought during World War II.

A movement among the towering reeds had caught their attention. Jesus M. Duenas unslung his hunting rifle, hoping for a wild pig. Instead, he saw a small, thin man making his way stealthily toward the river.

"A Japanese!" whispered Duenas to his companion, Manuel J. DeGracia. "Stop!" Duenas shouted.

The stranger stiffened and then dropped to his knees in prayer. As Duenas approached, the stranger sprang for the rifle desperately. But he was oddly weak and easily overpowered. His hands were quickly bound behind him.

The two men stepped back and studied

their captive. He was dressed in short pants and a short-sleeved shirt of tree bark; ragged, to be sure, yet cleverly tailored. His hair and beard were neatly trimmed.

Although relatives of both Duenas and DeGracia had been killed by Japanese soldiers during the war, neither man harmed their captive. They led him to Duenas's house, untied him, and fed him.

Gradually, he became less frightened. He spoke haltingly, as if he had not talked with anyone for so long that each word had to be remembered. Still, he made himself understood. He expected to be shot!

Duenas and DeGracia shook their heads and checked the calendar. It was the night of January 24 in the year 1972. The man seated before them was a Japanese soldier — a holdout from World War II!

They took him in their jeep to the village of Talofofo. From there he was removed to police headquarters at Agana, twenty miles away, and then to Guam Memorial Hospital.

Soon, newspapers seized upon his story. Headlines all over the world told how Shoichi Yokoi, a fifty-six-year-old army sergeant of the Imperial Japanese Army, had hidden in the jungles of Guam for twenty-eight years to escape capture!

When the Americans had retaken the island

in 1944, the Japanese officers had told their men that all prisoners would be shot. Yokoi believed them. For the last fifteen years of his concealment, he had lived in an underground cave which he had dug with pieces of a cannon shell. He never went out except at night and always stayed in the same area.

A tailor when drafted, Yokoi had made his own clothes and cut his hair and beard with a pair of scissors that he had carried through the war. The only other articles he kept from his army years were a waistband embroidered by his mother, and a Japanese flag.

For twenty-eight years he managed to survive on a diet of breadfruit, wild nuts, shrimp, snails, eels, and frogs. Only three times did he become seriously ill, once after tasting wild pig. He had been on his way to set shrimp traps when captured.

He had learned that the fighting on Guam was over from leaflets scattered in the jungle. But he held out, afraid he would be executed if he surrendered. About twenty years before his capture, he learned that the war had ended, but still he feared to come out of hiding.

Several other Japanese soldiers had hidden in the wilderness. His last two companions had died, probably of food poisoning, eight years earlier.

The day after his capture, Yokoi was still not free of fear. James Shintaku, the honorary Japanese consul on Guam, explained: "There is a Japanese military tradition that it is a disgrace to return home defeated."

"We Japanese soldiers were told to prefer death to the disgrace of being captured alive," said Yokoi.

Gradually, however, Yokoi relaxed. Members of the Japanese colony on Guam hurried to the hospital to see him. They approached him with polite murmurings of *"Gokuo sama"* (Thanks for your service), to which Yokoi replied, "Thanks."

Six days after his capture, Yokoi's half-brother, Osamu, and a cousin, Jotaro Sakai, visited him at the hospital. Yokoi learned that his mother had adopted Osamu after being told that Yokoi had died in the Marianas on September 30, 1944.

Sadly, Osamu could bring no news of Yokoi's fiancée. Before Yokoi was transferred by the army from Manchuria to Guam in 1943, his parents had arranged a marriage for him. But his leave to be wed was canceled. "I have no idea if she is even alive," Yokoi said forlornly.

While he regained his strength at Guam Memorial Hospital, letters and money poured in from well-wishers throughout Japan. The money totaled one hundred thousand yen, or three hundred and twenty-four dollars. Yokoi was overwhelmed.

"That will more than take care of me in style for the rest of my life," he said innocently. He had still to discover that three hundred and twenty-four dollars, a small fortune when he was young, would not keep him very long in 1972.

The army sergeant who had withdrawn from civilization at the age of twenty-eight was awed by the world he entered at fifty-six. He found color television and moon walks hard to believe, or that a jet could fly him home in three hours.

On February 2 a jet landed him at Tokyo International Airport, where he received a hero's welcome. A crowd of five thousand, waving little Japanese paper flags, greeted Yokoi with shouts of *"Banzai! Banzai!"* (Long Life!) Yokoi, seated in a wheelchair, waved his hands in response.

"This is like a dream to me," he said. "I am only afraid I shall wake up."

The Elevator Operator

Frederick Blackwood, the famous English diplomat known as Lord Dufferin, once saved his life because he recognized a ghost.

His encounter with the supernatural began while he was staying overnight at a friend's house in Ireland. He couldn't fall asleep, and all at once he was aware of something eerie, something he could not explain.

With senses sharply alert, he got out of bed and went to the window. Moonlight of unusual brightness flooded the grounds. He heard moaning.

He listened, tensing. There! It came again!

"I must get hold of myself," he thought. His mind shook off the stories he'd heard of haunted old Irish houses. "It is the breeze stirring in the trees."

31

The moaning grew steadily louder and closer. As Lord Dufferin squinted into the deep shadows cast by the huge ancient trees, he saw something move. Then he heard panting.

A man staggered from the shadows into the bright moonlight. He carried a long black box on his back, and he was moaning and panting under its weight.

Lord Dufferin left his room and hurried out onto the lawn. In the full moonlight he saw that the black box was a coffin.

"Hear," he called. "What are you doing with that?"

The man lifted his head from under his burden. Lord Dufferin saw his face and recoiled a step. It was a face so ugly and evil that he would never forget it.

Was the man a grave robber? Lord Dufferin nerved himself. "What are you doing with that?" he called again.

As he approached to within a few strides, the man and the coffin *disappeared before his eyes.*

Shaken, Lord Dufferin searched for signs of footprints in the dewy, moonlit grass. There were none.

Returning to his room, he wrote the details of the bewildering experience in his diary. When he laid down his pen, he believed

he had written an end to the matter — even if he would never forget that face!

But ended, the matter was not.

Years passed during which Lord Dufferin served England as ambassador to Italy and to Russia, and as governor-general of Canada. Then in 1891 he was named ambassador to France and in the city of Paris he met the ghost again.

The place was the Grand Hotel. Lord Dufferin stood waiting for an elevator to take him up to a reception. The other men in the lobby moved aside respectfully to let him enter first.

The door opened. Lord Dufferin started forward, then froze as he saw the elevator operator. How could he forget that ugly, evil face!

The operator was the same man he had seen carrying a coffin years before in Ireland — the man who had vanished into thin air! Calling upon all his self-control, Lord Dufferin betrayed no outward sign of terror.

To the others waiting, Lord Dufferin mumbled an excuse and bid them go ahead. As they crowded into the elevator, he rushed to the hotel office. He must know who the man was.

The crash sounded as he reached the office door. A cable had broken. The elevator had plunged five floors, killing everyone inside it.

At the insistence of Lord Dufferin, the secret services of England and France sought to learn the identity of the mysterious elevator operator.

Who was he? Where had he come from?

No one ever found out.

The Abominable Snowman

Is it possible that a lower form of man has existed on earth for millions of years?

In search of the answer, explorers and scientists have been drawn year after year to the snow-clad peaks of the Himalayas. From this chill and towering corner of the globe, lying between Tibet and India, have come fascinating rumors.

They concern a race of shaggy subhumans who make their homes on the forsaken slopes. The natives call them yeti, a name used for one or several of the snow creatures. Outsiders have another name, "abominable snowmen."

No foreigner has actually seen a yeti. Nonetheless, the natives have long lived in fear of them.

According to local accounts, a yeti is far stronger than a human being. He walks upright, has long arms, practically no neck, and huge feet. He goes without clothes and depends for warmth on his covering of dark reddish hair.

Despite his size, the yeti is considered shy. Seldom does he attack humans. It is said that if a man has the nerve to stand his ground, the creature will turn and flee.

The yeti supposedly eat small animals, insects, roots, and wild vegetables. They avoid civilization. Only when heavy snow makes food-gathering impossible on the upper slopes do they sneak near villages and steal cattle and sheep.

Perhaps the first outsider to see their mark was the mountaineer W. A. Waddel. In 1887 he claimed to have come across exceptionally large footprints in the snow. In 1913, Dr. V. A. Khaklov, a Russian scientist, gave a report on manlike beasts in the area. He was ridiculed and lost his professional standing.

Lt. Colonel Howard-Bury may have been the lone white man to glimpse a yeti. In 1921, while vainly trying to climb Mount Everest, he spied a darkish blob, moving rapidly across the snow at 16,000 feet. His guide and porters became terror-stricken, and the Englishman was never sure of what he had seen.

In May 1953, Sir Edmund Hillary, a New Zealander, conquered Mount Everest and found yeti footprints on the upward journey.

His native guide, Tenzing Norgay, said that his father, who never told lies, had once been chased by a yeti.

Since then many scientists and explorers have braved the treacherous slopes hoping to capture a yeti alive. They took along the latest in scientific equipment, including hypodermic air rifles designed to stun rather than kill.

The yeti remain as hard to find as ever. But at least their tracks have been located. Some of the expeditions have brought back photographs and plaster casts of five-toed footprints twice the size of a man's.

Today, investigation is being harmed by irresponsible "sightings" of yeti everywhere from Siberia to California. Pranksters and people dressed in elaborate costumes, so that they can be photographed for money, further confuse the search.

The natives of the Himalayas too have grown money-wise. They eagerly admit to having seen a yeti and do a brisk business selling "yeti" scalps, fur, and teeth — objects actually taken from such animals as yaks, snow leopards, and langurs.

Nawang Gombus, the only man to climb Mount Everest twice, said he heard the tiger-like scream of the yeti when he was growing up near the great mountain. But in 1967 he told reporters that he believed the yeti have gone the way of the dinosaur.

The range of guesswork, on who or what are the yeti, is wide and sometimes far-fetched. One group holds that the snow creatures are the livestock of people living inside the earth!

A major obstacle to finding the truth is the yeti homeland, the Himalayas. It is an area fifteen hundred miles long which varies from between sixty to one hundred miles wide. Called "the roof of the world," it contains five of the highest peaks on earth. Even to this day the region has many unexplored areas.

Its hiding places are many, and it keeps its secrets well.

Henry's Dowsing Rod

Bermuda was suffering one of its worst water shortages in history when Henry Gross arrived by plane late on the afternoon of December 5, 1949.

Since July, practically no rain had fallen. The islanders depended entirely on rain for their drinking water. Limewashed roofs and whitewashed rock rain-catchers trapped the rainfall and stored it in tanks. The tanks were running dry. The situation was critical.

Henry Gross, a stocky, mild-mannered man with thinning hair and spectacles, had never set foot on the island before. Yet he already knew where there was plenty of hidden water to be tapped.

The famed novelist Kenneth Roberts, an occasional resident of Bermuda, had summoned Henry. Both men made their homes in Maine. Roberts had frequently used Henry's special gifts to find fresh water springs on his farm.

Now Roberts wanted Henry to find water in Bermuda with his dowsing rod — a forked branch.

The experts insisted there was no water to be found. Trained geologists laid the absence of fresh water and rivers to Bermuda's natural rock formation of porous limestone.

To be sure, Bermuda had several wells. They yielded brackish water fit for irrigation, cooking, and bathroom use. But absolutely no fresh water.

Despite the weight of this "expert" opinion, Roberts and Henry Gross were confident of success. They had their reasons. The previous October at the Roberts' farm in Maine, eight hundred miles away from Bermuda, Henry had dowsed four Bermuda wells.

It had happened like this: One evening Roberts brought up the subject of Bermuda's constant water problem to Henry after dinner, and Henry's curiosity was aroused. That night, using a forked branch and a small map of the island, Henry located fresh water springs in Devonshire Parish, Smith's Parish, and the Royal Barracks.

There was a fourth well, in St. George's Parish, he said, but it was polluted.

Now actually on Bermuda Island, Henry's dowsing rod pinpointed the long-distance findings of the previous October. The results,

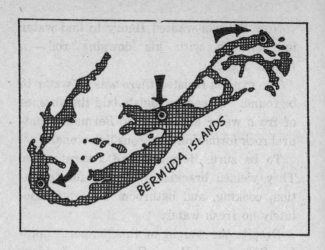

BERMUDA ISLANDS

however, were not to be known for six months.

Government leaders declined to give their approval to a "switch-twitcher." From the start, the work of digging dragged under the double load of bungling and uncooperative officials.

Pure water might be struck by chance, the officials allowed, but it would be merely a few gallons of drainage. After a bit more pumping, the wells would prove to be like all the others, brackish and undrinkable.

Week after week Roberts battled to get the right drills, the right pumps, and trained workmen to bring up the water Henry Gross said was there. Roberts beat himself raw against the walls of indifference and suspicion.

A ship brought an emergency supply of water. While tank trucks rumbled over the island, while the poor used their precious water sparingly and the rich bought theirs on the black market, all the fresh water Bermuda needed — Roberts was positive — flowed underground.

Henry Gross returned to Maine on December 13, 1949, and once more was dowsing for anyone who asked him.

His talents with a dowsing rod were perhaps the best developed in the country. Yet his method was simple. First he cut a forked tree branch to make his dowsing rod. Then gripping a forked end in each hand, he slowly turned in a circle till the rod pointed with a pull on his hands to the underground vein.

The next step was to establish the distance of the vein. "Is it two hundred feet?" he would ask. The rod answered "yes" by dipping in his grasp. "Is it three hundred feet?" The rod answered "no" by remaining still. That meant that the vein would be between two and three hundred feet away. Through further questioning, he would narrow the distance down to the exact foot.

With the presence of water confirmed and the vein located and traced, he put other questions to the dowsing rod. It responded by dipping or remaining still. He determined the depth of the vein, how many gallons flowed per minute, and whether the water was pure enough to drink.

He dowsed hundreds of wells, and Kenneth Roberts never knew him to fail. "If his stick indicates an underground well, the water's there," declared Roberts flatly.

In May, Henry received news from Bermuda. The wells had come in just as he had said they would! The Bermudians, however, avoided openly acknowledging their debt to him.

Henry was pleased, anyway. He often helped folks in Maine find water and got paid no more than five dollars. And if he wasn't paid for finding water in Bermuda, he at least had the satisfaction of knowing he was right.

Lincoln and Kennedy

Soon after the assassination of President John F. Kennedy, believers in the supernatural started turning up facts that likened his life — and death — to that of Abraham Lincoln.

Is there a fateful connection between the two martyred Presidents? Consider the following.

Both served their country in war; Lincoln in the Black Hawk War, Kennedy in World War II.

Both gained political stature through debates; Lincoln with Stephen A. Douglas, Kennedy with Richard M. Nixon.

Both were elected to Congress in a year ending in 47; Lincoln in 1847, Kennedy a hundred years later in 1947.

Both were elected President in a year ending in 60; Lincoln in 1860, Kennedy a hundred years later in 1960.

Both were succeeded by Vice Presidents named Johnson, who had been United States senators.

Lincoln had a secretary named Kennedy who tried to stop him from going to Ford's Theater; Kennedy had a secretary named Lincoln who tried to stop him from going to Dallas.

Both were assassinated on Friday.

Both were shot in the back of the head.

Both were seated next to their wives when they were slain.

Both Johnsons were born in the South.

John Wilkes Booth and Lee Harvey Oswald, the assassins, were both born in the South.

Andrew Johnson was born in 1808; Lyndon Johnson was born a hundred years later in 1908.

Booth was born in 1839; Oswald was born a hundred years later in 1939.

Booth and Oswald were each shot to death before they could stand trial.

Booth shot Lincoln in a theater and fled to

a storehouse, a farmer's barn. Oswald shot Kennedy from a storehouse, a book repository, and fled to a theater.

The names John Wilkes Booth and Lee Harvey Oswald have fifteen letters each.

The names Andrew Johnson and Lyndon Johnson have thirteen letters each.

The names Lincoln and Kennedy have seven letters each.

Another Jonah

"There she blows!"

The whaling ship *Star of the East* was plowing through the South Atlantic off the Falkland Islands when the cry lifted. Ahead loomed the spout of a sperm whale, and — as yet unseen — the most singular of sea miracles since Biblical times.

Sails were set on the square-rigger and pursuit began. In half an hour the *Star of the East* closed to striking range. Immediately a pair of twenty-five-foot boats were launched.

When the lead boat reached within a few yards of the whale, the harpooner aimed the new-fangled spear gun. The point sank home in the blubbery side.

The whale thrashed in pain. Sixty feet of sea-monster, weighing a ton a foot, rolled and twisted, its powerful tail slamming the ocean.

The violent churning lifted the second boat and flipped her over, tossing the crew into the water. Terrified, they clung to the overturned

hull till the whale was killed and they could be rescued.

All were accounted for save two. One of the missing men was known to have drowned. The other was James Bartley, twenty-one, an English sailor making his first voyage aboard the *Star of the East*.

Captain Wedderman entered the names of both men dutifully in the log and after each name wrote, "Drowned." During the frenzy of the accident, no one could be sure just when or how James Bartley had disappeared.

The matter of the unfortunate seamen was quickly laid aside, for there was urgent work to do. The whale was tied to the ship. Using razor-sharp flensing spades, the men sliced and peeled the heavy blubber.

At midnight work stopped. The exhausted men went below and slept till dawn, when they rose and returned to their work.

The stomach was hoisted onto the deck.

Inside was a large lump. The men thought at first that the lump was ambergris, a waxy substance found in whales and used in making the finest perfumes.

They were startled to see the lump move ... slow movements like breathing ...

Captain Wedderman was summoned, and he looked on as a long cut was made in the tissue. A shoe appeared ... and an ankle. Inside the whale's stomach was the missing sailor James Bartley, doubled up and unconscious — but alive!

He bore only one outward sign of his ordeal: His skin was pasty white from the whale's digestive juices. A bath from a few buckets of icy sea water revived his body but not his reason. He let out a howl, staggered blindly, struck the railing, and collapsed.

He was carried to the captain's quarters. For two weeks he lay strapped to the bunk, a raving lunatic. Gradually he recovered his senses. After a month he resumed work.

Bartley described his feelings on that horrible day in February 1891 to Captain Wedderman and later to a board of inquiry of the British Admiralty.

He remembered being hurled into the ocean. Suddenly he was surrounded by absolute darkness. He slid along a smooth passage that seemed to carry him forward. His hands touched a soft, slimy substance. He could breathe, but the heat was dreadful. (A whale's blood is 104.6 degrees Fahrenheit.) He recalled nothing more until he woke up in the captain's cabin.

When the *Star of the East* returned to port, James Bartley quit the sea. The modern Jonah lived eighteen more years, which he spent as a cobbler in his native Gloucester.

Potemkin's Villages

The movies have never known a producer to equal the talents of Gregory Potemkin. Yet he did not make one picture.

He made a country.

He built pretty villages with little more than cardboard and paint. He peopled them with dancing peasants who were hurried from place to place a step ahead of their unsuspecting audience.

He did it all to make the woman he loved happy. She was Empress Catherine the Great of Russia, and they may have been secretly married. No one knows for sure. In 1783 Catherine had acquired the Crimea. She appointed Potemkin governor of the area. His job was to turn the barren land into thriving country.

Potemkin went to work with a will and a vast imagination. He promised Catherine hundreds of improvements, and in the next three years made several trips north to the capital to report his successes. Catherine was thrilled with his words. She must see for herself!

Potemkin had not made a wasteland bloom. He had, however, created the *appearance* of lush countryside for Catherine's pleasure. When Catherine expressed a desire to see it he hastened ahead to make final arrangements.

Catherine set out on her tour of the Crimea in a sledge—a heavy sleighlike, horse-drawn platform. It was the size of a small house, and the empress took forty thousand followers with her. At every station along the route five hundred fresh horses were waiting.

And at every station, Catherine stared in delight. Houses had been repainted — on the side facing her — and roofs repaired — with cardboard. Young girls strewed flowers in her path; old and sickly people had been locked indoors. Artificial trees blocked unsightly areas. Begging was forbidden. Everyone, Potemkin had ordered, must "express happiness by smiles and gestures."

Years before, Catherine had traveled the same road. She had seen the misery and the angry faces. She was overcome by the change.

"Is not my little household prettily furnished?" she gasped to the French ambassador.

All this was but a taste of what was to come. The real journey through Potemkin's fairyland began at the Dnieper River. Seven floating palaces trailed by eighty smaller vessels carried three thousand persons past never-ending wonders.

While Catherine and her royal party lay under silken awnings and dined on plates of gold, a storybook landscape streamed by: villages decorated with triumphal arches ... cattle grazing contentedly ... carefree peasants dancing at dusk.

Catherine could not guess the truth: that the wonderland vanished behind her.

The triumphal arches were shakily thrown up. Farmhouses were without real roofs, windows, or doors. The villages were deserted. The cattle had been brought great distances without feed to make them graze "contentedly." The "carefree" dancers were poor peasants, taught their steps by threats and beatings. They were packed into carts and carried farther down the river to perform the next evening.

Potemkin had spared no cost. At the three anchorages along the river he had built a splendid new palace with every luxury. Each was adorned with a man-made waterfall and a park shaded by transplanted trees that withered and died after Catherine had departed.

Leaving the river, the empress traveled by carriage through villages alive with industry and smiling crowds. She had no way of knowing that Potemkin had whisked in every peasant for miles around to flesh out his roadside landscape.

At Ekaterinoslav, Catherine laid the cornerstone of a cathedral whose plans made St. Peter's in Rome look like a chapel. At Kherson she viewed from afar a huge new fortress. At Sevastopol, while one hundred and eighty musicians played at dinner, she looked out over the harbor at her new Black Sea fleet of warships. Potemkin had built the fleet in two years. The deck guns fired a salute.

The climax came at Poltava. Potemkin staged a mock battle that reenacted the victory of Peter the Great on the same ground.

Catherine went back to her capital singing Potemkin's praises. The Crimea had been turned into the pride of all Russia! She died without ever learning that the beautiful land was an invention of the man she loved and who loved her — and the greatest hoax in history!

The cathedral at Ekaterinoslav was never built. The fleet of warships had been clapped together of such poor material that it could never see action. Its guns fired powder only; there were no shells. The huge fortress of Kherson was constructed of sand, and collapsed after the first thunderstorm!

Rex

During the first half of the twentieth century no American writer of dog stories was better loved than Albert Payson Terhune.

One of his favorite pets was a mongrel dog, Rex, who was almost as big as a Great Dane. Rex had a short, light brown coat and a scar across his forehead.

Rex loved his master and would lie for hours at Terhune's feet, looking up at his face. If Terhune moved about, Rex would follow quietly, lying down again when the writer settled himself.

Rex was not allowed in the dining room. So he went out on the porch and stood looking at Terhune through the French windows. He was not allowed in the writer's study, either. He always lay down in one special spot outside the study door. It was his only regular resting place.

Rex died in March 1916. Terhune wrote

about his death in his book *Lad: A Dog*. The next year Terhune's old friend, the Rev. Appleton Grannis, paid him a visit. Grannis had not been in Terhune's home in many years. They dined together.

As they were leaving the table, Grannis said, "I thought I knew all your dogs. But there's one I never saw till now. The large dog with the short, light brown coat and the scarred forehead.

Terhune shook his head. "We don't have a short-haired dog," he replied. "Or one with a scar across his forehead."

"But," protested Grannis, "the dog was standing outside the window looking at you all the time we were eating. He's disappeared now. What's his name?"

Terhune answered truthfully. "I don't know."

Henry A. Healy used to visit Terhune often. Healy was interested in crossbreeding, and he had made a study of Rex.

In the autumn of 1918, the Terhunes had the Healys to dinner. Afterward, they sat talking by firelight. The hour grew late. The Healys rose to bid good night.

"I wish there were a creature as devoted to me as Rex is to you," Healy remarked to Terhune. "I was observing him as he lay in the firelight at your feet. He stared into your face with a queer kind of worship. He must — "

"Good heavens!" Terhune interrupted. "Rex died more than two years ago!"

Healy frowned in confusion. "Of course . . . I know . . . Yet, I swear he was lying at your feet all evening."

A collie named Bruce was the only Terhune dog allowed in the study. After Rex died, Bruce never once stepped on the patch of floor outside the study door where Rex used to lie.

During the four years in which Bruce outlived Rex, the collie always walked around the spot, as if avoiding an invisible object.

Time and again Terhune put Bruce to the test before guests. When he called the dog into the study, Bruce always took the strange little detour.

Why?

Terhune did not know. He did not believe in ghosts, dog or human. Still . . .

"How did Grannis chance to see a dog peering through the window at me?" he said. "Grannis never heard of Rex. Healy is a level-headed businessman, not given to fancies. What did he see lying at my feet in the firelight?"

Terhune could only guess.

Jack the Ripper

Between August 6 and November 9, 1888, five women were murdered in London. Their deaths were similar, marking them as the victims of the same killer.

Because of the horrible way he used his knife, the unknown assailant was dubbed Jack the Ripper.

For eighty-two years no criminal commanded such a tireless hold upon the imagination of the world. Jack the Ripper was the subject of countless magazine articles and stories. His dark deeds were enacted in motion pictures, television, and opera.

He chose his victims from the street. He gained their confidence and was even seen talking to them. Eyewitness descriptions of him were in agreement: He wore a deerstalker's hat and "talked like a gentleman."

Yet the mysterious "gentleman" was never caught.

He struck five times in three months and then struck no more. Who was he? How did he escape capture when he taunted the police, challenging them to find him? He boasted in writing of his murders before and after he committed them.

When Sir Charles Warren, chief of Scotland Yard, arrived at one of the murder scenes, he saw writing — obviously the killer's — chalked on a wall nearby. He ordered it erased immediately. Why? Was not the writing a clue?

The public wondered.

Were the police really baffled, *or were they covering up?* Rumors grew with the passing years. The killer who talked like a gentleman ... was importantly placed in government ... he was of royal blood!

The rumors held scraps of truth. But the whole truth was more incredible than anyone had dared imagine.

Jack the Ripper was no mere officeholder. He was no minor member of the royal family far down the line of succession.

To his immediate circle of friends and relatives he was "Eddy." To the public he was Albert Victor Christian Edward, Duke of Clarence and Avondale, and a favorite of his grandmother Victoria, Queen of England!

His father was Prince of Wales, later King Edward VII. His sister Maud was the future Queen of Norway. His younger brother became George V.

In 1970, seventy-nine years after his death, Eddy was exposed as Jack the Ripper. Dr. Thomas Stowell had known the shocking truth for fifty years. He withheld it deliberately. He did not wish to involve as witnesses close friends who were still living.

As a young man Dr. Stowell studied under Sir William Gull, the royal physician. Dr. Gull had a daughter, Caroline, who snooped in her father's diary and passed along choice tidbits to young Dr. Stowell.

Dr. Gull had treated Eddy for a disease which had steadily sapped the duke's physical and mental strength. After four murders, Eddy was placed in a private mental hospital. He escaped and murdered for the fifth and last time.

After that Sir Charles Warren resigned as chief of Scotland Yard. His conscience did not permit him to continue in office while hushing up England's worst-ever murderer.

For a while Eddy showed signs of recovering. He went on a five-month cruise, but he died in 1891, a few weeks after his return. The official cause of death was listed as pneumonia. He was twenty-eight.

Had he lived until his father, King Edward VII, died in 1910, Eddy and not his younger brother George might have sat upon the throne. The most infamous criminal in history might have ruled the British Empire!

The Incredible Painting

The rough and tumble rivermen at Louisville did not know what to make of the young artist. He walked right up and urged them to see a *painting*.

"It's your river I have painted," declared John Banvard. He pressed free tickets on any of the rivermen who seemed mildly interested. "You owe it to yourselves and the Mississippi River to come and see it."

A former peddler, Banvard used all his powers of salesmanship on the rivermen. A few showed up at his exhibition the next night. What they saw amazed them.

For Banvard was as good as his word. He had painted the Mississippi River "in every detail" — on a canvas *three miles long!*

Banvard was twenty-five when he undertook the largest painting in the world. In 1840 he began four hundred days of travel down the Mississippi River in a skiff, making sketches.

Next he built a studio back in Louisville, large enough to double as an exhibition hall. There he labored eighteen hours a day for six years, painting the scenes on a canvas especially woven for the purpose at Lowell, Massachusetts.

In 1846 the mammoth task was completed. The following year Banvard was ready to exhibit. But on opening night not a soul came. The second night was the same. Banvard despaired. He thought he had wasted seven years of his life.

So he went down to the docks and persuaded the rivermen to have a look. The rivermen told their friends. The next night the hall was jammed. Banvard's reputation was made.

To show his *Panorama of the Mississippi*, he used two upright rollers. The canvas passed between them like a scroll. Banvard lectured with a pointer as the canvas slowly unwound. It took two hours for the entire picture to be seen.

Viewers had the feeling that they were taking a leisurely trip down twelve hundred miles of river country, from the mouth of the Missouri River to New Orleans. In a sense, the "Panorama" was America's first motion picture.

The chief merit of the painting was geographic. As a work of art, it had little value. But its popularity was enormous. It was shown across the United States, and in London before an admiring Queen Victoria.

Banvard realized two hundred thousand dollars from admissions. And the "Panorama" made him famous as the artist who painted a canvas three miles long — the largest painting ever.

The Tumbling Dead

Do the dead rest in peace?

Ask the people of the island of Barbados, British West Indies. They shake their heads and point to an abandoned vault in the graveyard of Christ Church.

Nothing unusual happened to the first three coffins placed in the vault. That came later.

Mrs. Thomasina Goddard was buried in July 1807. She was followed a year later by Mary Anna Chase, age two. On July 6, 1812, the coffin of Dorcas Chase, an older sister of Mary Anna, joined the pair.

Then, four weeks afterward, Thomas Chase, head of the Chase family, died. When the vault was opened, the burial party stepped back in shock.

Two of the coffins had moved!

That of little Mary Anna stood head downward in a corner. That of Mrs. Goddard lay on its side against a wall.

The coffins were replaced in their original positions on the floor and Thomas Chase's was added to the row.

The vault was opened next on September 15, 1816, to receive the coffin of Samuel Brewster Ames, age 11 months. It had happened again! The coffins were tumbled about!

Fifty-two days later the vault was opened to admit the infant's father, Samuel Brewster. *Again!*

By now the governor of Barbados, Lord Combermere, had become concerned about the restless coffins. He decided to be present at the next burial.

On July 17, 1819, he stood beside the vault to watch Mrs. Thomazina Clarke laid to rest. With him were his staff, most of the island's clergymen, and hundreds of spectators.

The cement around the heavy slab that closed the entrance was chipped away and the slab hoisted clear. Then — the governor saw with his own eyes — the coffins had been tumbled this way and that!

The governor did not believe in voodoo or poltergeists. Pranksters were responsible, he declared.

He took charge. The walls of the vault were sounded for weaknesses and hidden entrances. The surrounding ground was inspected for tunnels. The search was in vain.

There was no way a living human could enter the vault.

A heavy layer of sand was spread over the floor of the vault. The marble slab was lifted back over the entrance and cemented down. Then the governor and four other men pressed their private seals into the wet cement. Whoever tried to sneak into the vault now would have to break the impressions of the seals and leave footprints in the sand. The governor was satisfied.

And yet the vault preyed on his mind. Finally, on April 18, 1820, he could bear the waiting no longer.

That afternoon he visited the graveyard with three aides and the Rev. Thomas Ordeson, Rector of Christ Church. The men examined the cement around the entrance slab. The seals were unbroken.

Two masons loosed the heavy slab. Four slaves pushed it aside. The governor peered in. The sand on the floor was without footprints or marks.

But the vault was in chaos!

A child's coffin lay on the steps leading to the chamber. The other coffins were turned upside down, except that of Mrs. Goddard, which was untouched.

The governor gave up. There was absolutely no way anyone could have invaded the fortresslike vault.

If you visit Barbados, you can see the vault for yourself. It is built of large blocks of coral rock cemented together and sunk two feet into the limestone ground. It is windowless and probably airtight. Within, it measures twelve feet by six and a half feet.

What had moved the coffins?

Grave robbers? How? Besides, nothing of value was buried with the dead, and none of the lids had been pried.

Floods? Several coffins were made of wood encased in lead, making them tremendously heavy. Lead coffins have been known to float, but there were no water marks on the walls or reports of flooding in other parts of the graveyard.

Earthquakes? An earthquake might have shifted the coffins. But no quake had shaken the area. Even if quakes had struck this one tiny spot and nowhere else, could they have struck *five times*?

The governor ordered the coffins removed and buried in another cemetery. Ever since then, the vault has stood empty.

The Man Who
Didn't Hang

"Will Purvis," the sheriff said in a tone-less voice, "do you have any last words?"

The young farmer on the platform straightened. His hands were tied behind him; his ankles were roped together. He looked down upon the crowd assembled in Court House Square, Columbia, Mississippi.

"I am innocent," he declared. "I did not kill Will Buckley. There are men among you who could save me if they wanted to."

The sheriff placed the black hood over Purvis's head and made fast the noose around his neck. The crowd let out a shout as the trap door sprang open and his body shot downward.

It was February 7, 1894, and, as everyone believed, the last split-second of Will Purvis's twenty-one years of life.

Suddenly the shouts changed to screams. The empty noose had bounced in the air and was dancing above the open trap door. Will Purvis lay on the ground below, still hooded and bound — and still breathing!

"I heard the door squeak, and I dropped down and everything went black," he remembered. "When I woke up, somebody gripping me said, 'I guess we've got to do it all over again.'"

Two sheriff's deputies lugged him up the steps of the scaffold to be hanged once more.

As the noose slipped over his head again, the Rev. W. S. Sibley of the Columbia Methodist Church bounded onto the platform.

"Good people!" he cried. "The hand of the Lord has touched the noose. Can we let Will Purvis be hanged again?"

The people shouted, "No! No!" They had beheld a miracle, and they rejoiced and chanted the praises of the Lord.

The sheriff read their mood. He knew that if he tried to hang Purvis again, the crowd would surge onto the scaffold and overpower him. He led the prisoner back to jail.

Had a miracle saved Will Purvis's life? It would seem so.

A noose tied with a hangman's knot cannot possibly be placed around a man's neck in a way to allow his head to slip free as his body falls. If the knot does slip, the noose only becomes tighter.

Moreover, the sheriff believed Purvis was guilty. He had done his best to carry out the sentence of the court.

The governor did not believe in miracles, however. He ordered Purvis to be hanged again.

Public feeling ran strongly against the order. Officials took notice. They granted a remarkable favor. Purvis was moved from the sturdy Columbia jail to a flimsy one in his hometown so that he could be near his friends in the last days of his life.

Purvis had many friends. A few days before the date of the second hanging, a mob broke into the jail and rescued him. Nobody, including the officials, was much surprised.

It was no secret that Purvis hid out with kinfolk after his escape. Yet he was never turned in, despite tempting rewards offered by the angry governor.

Then a new governor took office. He altered the sentence to life imprisonment. Purvis gave himself up. He found that the people had not forgotten him. They still believed God had overruled the jury. Thousands signed a petition asking for his freedom. He was pardoned after serving twenty-two months.

He bought a small farm with the help of friends, married a preacher's daughter, and raised eleven children. And when he was forty-seven, something akin to a second miracle entered his life.

Joe Beard, an old planter, confessed on his deathbed to the crime for which Purvis had been "hanged." Beard, and another member of a gang known as the White Caps, had shot Will Buckley from ambush.

"God heard my prayers that day I went to the gallows," said Purvis. "He saved my life because I was innocent."

The Girl Who Fell
Six Miles

The explosion ripped the air high above the Bohemian mountain region of northern Czechoslovakia.

Villagers looked up in alarm. They could make out a jet airliner six miles above them, but not the raw hole blown in its luggage compartment.

The plane, a Yugoslav DC-9 on a regular flight from Stockholm and Copenhagen to Zagreb and Belgrade, flew on for a few seconds before other explosions tore it apart.

A horrifying rain of wreckage and bodies hurtled down. Twisted steel and victims were scattered over miles of the forested countryside.

The tail section plunged into a snowy, wooded slope. A game warden named Henke reached the spot first.

Nothing, he reasoned, could have survived

the crash. He saw several bodies. Then, to his astonishment, he heard a feeble moan.

Lying in the snow was a blonde girl in a dark uniform. She was Vesna Vulovic, twenty-three, a stewardess.

Henke wisely made no attempt to move her. He covered her unconscious form with his coat and hurried for help. An ambulance rushed her to the hospital, where she underwent a three-hour operation. Dr. Miloslav Randa was the surgeon.

Vesna regained consciousness briefly. She was able to speak her name and give the number of her flight. The following day she recognized her mother, who had come from Belgrade.

With Mrs. Vulovic was Dr. Dragoslav Adamovic. He conferred with Dr. Randa. The two surgeons decided to transfer Vesna to Prague by helicopter for neurosurgery.

In Prague specialists removed a piece of vertebra that was pressing on Vesna's spinal cord. The operation succeeded, and slowly Vesna recovered.

But she could remember nothing of falling thirty-two thousand feet. The terrible seconds of January 26, 1972, were a blank. Doctors considered this lapse in her memory a blessing. The shock of recall might have affected her mind.

Investigators studied the wreckage as well as voice and flight records. The evidence was clear. The first explosion had been caused by a time bomb hidden in the luggage compartment. Instruments registered an explosion during a conversation between the pilot and a stewardess. Up to that moment, everything in the jetliner had been working normally.

Unanswered was the question of how Vesna Vulovic had lived when everyone else aboard — all twenty-two passengers and the crew of four — was killed.

What had taken the lives of many of the passengers was the sudden loss of air pressure inside the cabin. They had died strapped in their seats.

Vesna's survival is a matter of guesswork, assisted by something she muttered after her spinal operation. She mentioned oxygen masks and fretted at not being able to help anyone.

Fitting her remarks into the known facts, investigators put together the chain of events surrounding Vesna's miraculous escape from death.

The explosion occurred when the passengers were due to be served a meal. Consequently, Vesna was on her feet.

During the ghastly moments of flight between the first explosion and the break-up of the crippled plane, the passengers screamed for breath. Vesna scrambled for the oxygen masks — masks were found near where she and the tail section came to earth.

As she tried one on, the tail section broke off. The pretty stewardess was thrown into a corner and knocked unconscious. Her physical system was thus slowed, and she was relaxed during the fall.

With Vesna inside, the tail section struck a pine-covered hillside. The treetops cushioned the impact. Vesna was hurled clear and slid down the hill, further reducing the impact.

She had come through explosions, decompression, the fall, and the crash — and lived!

The name of Vesna Vulovic, the girl who fell six miles, is imprinted upon medical history as one of the greatest examples of the durability of the human body.

The Piri Re'is Map

Was our planet mapped thousands of years ago by a people more advanced perhaps than we are?

The question arises because an old map, redrawn by a Turkish officer, Admiral Piri Re'is, was found in the Imperial Palace in Istanbul, Turkey, in 1929.

The map is fairly accurate. But what is startling is that it shows islands, valleys, rivers, and bays along the coast of Antarctica, the land that surrounds the South Pole.

How was this done? The Antarctic coast lies buried under hundreds of feet of ice. Today maps of the region are drawn by bouncing echoes off the land below the ice.

Scientists believe that ice has coated Antarctica for thousands of years. Yet *someone* mapped the coast through the great depths of ice, or lived before ice covered the continent!

The Piri Re'is map is drawn on the skin of

a gazelle. It is dated 1513. But Piri Re'is himself wrote that it was copied from other maps which he thought were drawn as far back as 356 B.C.

Experts think the original maps must have been made long, long before then. We know map makers copied from earlier maps, and then copies were made of copies. Some errors in Piri Re'is's map may be explained as the fault of the copyists over the centuries. Other differences can be blamed on the rising level of the oceans. Slowly, over great periods of time, the water rose and changed coastlines and sank islands.

Nevertheless, the accuracy of the Piri Re'is map of 1513 and of others copied by him are amazing. Who *first* drew them? Whoever did must have used sophisticated instruments and known a great deal about mathematics.

These mysterious map makers of prehistory are called "ancient sea kings" by Professor Charles Hapgood, who has carefully studied the 1513 map. He believes the sea kings lived at least five thousand years ago.

What became of them, this race of sea kings? Were they really sailors? Did they really go with the wind to all points of the globe? Did they put out on tremendous voyages when other men feared to venture beyond the sight of land? How could they vanish so utterly — as if they simply flew off the earth, taking their ships with them?

Perhaps they did in fact fly off the earth. The originals of the Piri Re'is map would then have been aerial photographs taken from a great height.

Ponder the evidence.

The ancient Egyptian city of Alexandria is located on the central line of longitude on the map of 1513. Imagine that thousands of years ago a spaceship hovered above Alexandria and aimed its camera directly down on the city.

The developed film would show everything within a radius of a few thousand miles of Alexandria in correct shape. But bodies of land and water would appear more and more misshapen the farther they were from Alexandria, the center of the photograph.

Why? Because the earth is round. The continents and seas away from the center appear increasingly distorted, just as they do on Piri Re'is's maps — and just as they do on photographs taken from space by satellites and the Apollo moon flights!

Not "sea kings" in sailing vessels, but *visitors from outer space* may have taken the photographs on which the Piri Re'is maps are based.

There are things in ancient times which

still cannot be explained by modern scholars. Suppose visitors from space gave their aerial photographs to mankind. And before flying home they performed other feats which have come down to us through the mists of time as historical puzzles.

For example, who really built the pyramid of Cheops? Who designed Stonehenge? Is that a prehistoric airfield in the Andes? How to account for an electric battery thousands of years old?

Our earth teems with hundreds of such puzzles — miracles impossible to primitive man. But seen in a new light, who can say that the Piri Re'is map is not among the many clues telling us that once, thousands of years ago, the earth was visited by superior beings from a distant planet?

L-8

To the mysteries of the sky add the case of the L-8.

Since the dawn of aviation, aircraft have flown into the clouds never to be seen again. The L-8 disappeared into the clouds all right. Thereafter, her story is like no other.

She reappeared and eventually came to earth — *without her crew!*

During World War II the L-8, a Navy blimp, patrolled the California coast near San Francisco. At 6 A.M., August 16, 1942, she took off from the Treasure Island Naval base on a routine flight.

Aboard was her two-man crew, Lieutenant (j.g.) Ernest D. Cody and Ensign Charles F. Adams of Airship Squadron 32. The day was overcast. A light rain fell intermittently.

Almost two hours later, Lt. Cody radioed the control tower at the base, "Am investigating large oil slick." He gave his position as five miles east of the Farallon Islands.

The message aroused no concern. Oil slicks were common and did not necessarily mean an enemy submarine lurked underwater.

Two fishing craft and two patrol boats, one Navy and the other Coast Guard, were near the oil slick when the blimp began circling at a height of three hundred feet. The fishing boats hurried to a respectful distance in case the L-8 dropped depth bombs.

Bombs were not dropped. Instead, the L-8 suddenly soared into the clouds. The men on the four ships watched her disappear. They did not see her again.

Some fifteen minutes had passed since the tower had received Lt. Cody's radio message. At 8:05 A.M. an attempt was made to contact the blimp. The L-8 did not reply. Immediately two OS2U Kingfisher search planes flew to investigate.

At 10:30 A.M. a Pan American Airways clipper reported the blimp south of the Golden Gate Bridge. At 10:40 A.M. one of the Kingfishers sighted her as she rose briefly above the clouds.

Moments later viewers at Fort Funston saw her wander in from the ocean and strike the beach a mile away. A pair of surf fishermen tried to grab the loose lines and tie her down. They noticed the gondola door was open: No one was inside. A gust of wind tore the airship from their hands.

The L-8 struck a cliff near the beach and one of the depth bombs fell alongside a highway, unexploded. Lightened, the blimp sailed off. At 11:15 A.M., her helium bag leaking, she landed on a street in Daly City, south of San Francisco.

Navy experts examined the wreck. They found nothing amiss in the gondola. Rubber life raft, parachutes, and documents were in place. The radio was turned "on," but the battery had run down. The throttle to one motor was wide open, the other half open.

Missing were the two airmen and the bright yellow life jackets they were required to wear when over water.

The landing space below the deck of the gondola, which contained control wires, was dry. From this the experts reasoned that the blimp had not touched down on the ocean.

Had Cody and Adams fallen while circling above the oil slick? The loss of their weight might explain the blimp's sudden zoom into the clouds.

But then, surely their falling bodies or the splashes would have been seen by the men on the four boats nearby. Even if the two officers had been knocked loose from their life jackets upon hitting the surface, the jackets themselves should have been found floating.

And would not the bodies of Cody and Adams have eventually washed ashore.

At a naval hearing, witnesses from the four boats said they had seen neither splashes nor men falling. A full-scale search failed to find a trace of the life jackets or the missing airmen.

Only this much is known:

Whatever happened to Cody and Adams took place in the fifteen minutes between their last radio message and the unsuccessful attempt by the tower to contact them.

During those fifteen minutes, the L-8 was either circling the oil slick or hidden from sight in the clouds.

The Loch Ness Monster

If you are interested in sea monsters, visit a lake in the highlands of Scotland named Loch Ness.

Don't go between June and September, however. That is "monster season." Crowds descend from all over the world. Hotels are booked solid, and boats must be hired well in advance.

The canny Scots of the region have used the monster to build a spanking tourist trade. All year round you can buy souvenirs — buttons, postcards, handkerchiefs, spy glasses, even bikinis — with monster pictures.

But Loch Ness offers more than hotels, souvenir shops, and ballyhoo. In all probability there *is* a monster in the lake. Watch long enough, and you may see large lumps break surface out on the slate-gray lake.

Legends of a monster in Loch Ness date back to ancient times. Modern interest began on November 12, 1933, when Hugh Gray saw an awesome shape roll up from the deep and as suddenly disappear.

Soon hosts of men and women reported seeing the monster. The public was aroused. In July 1934, Sir Edward Mountain organized a group of 20 men with field glasses to stand watch throughout the year.

Later, scientists and amateurs formed the Loch Ness Phenomenon Investigation Bureau, Limited. The Bureau keeps a technician stationed at the lake. During the summer, he is assisted by members with field glasses and long-range cameras.

Thousands of pictures have been taken by the Bureau and by sightseers. The results are disappointing. Not one has been clear and detailed. For some reason, the monster simply will not hold still and pose.

The most famous snapshot was taken in 1934. It is generally held to be a fake. It shows a serpent's head set on a long slender neck sticking straight up from the water.

The serpent's head and long neck are commonly reported features. A composite of the other features most frequently described provides a rough portrait. The mysterious creature is ninety feet long, six feet wide, and six feet high. It has eight short legs, a fifteen-foot tail, and five or six humps that

appear atop the surface like a chain of over-turned boats.

The nature of Loch Ness rules out any close-up, scientific study. The lake is twenty-three miles long, a mile wide, and ranges to a depth of seven hundred and fifty-four feet, twice that of the North Sea. Seepage from peat bogs has drained into the water so that it is impossible to see down more than a few feet. Scuba divers and windowed submarines would poke blindly about the darkness and great depths.

The Bureau's monster-watchers have made several hundred genuine sightings over the past few years. What is the humped brute they see from a distance? Guesses are as numerous as guessers and cover a crocodile, a whale, a tree trunk, a sea lion, a tortoise. Experts lean toward a giant type of sea slug or snail.

For the supporters of a real monster, geologists hold out this possibility: They believe that Loch Ness once connected with the sea. Did prehistoric marine animals, drawn by the cold depths, swim into Loch Ness before the earth changed and the passageway closed?

If that is what happened, the rest of the story is easy to piece together. The trapped monsters thrived and bred. Meanwhile, others of their kind — those still in the oceans — gradually died out.

So the Loch Ness monsters lived thousands of years after nature intended them to vanish. Not one, but many of them may be rising up to peek at a world in which they no longer belong.

One quick peek may be all it takes to drive them back to the safety of Loch Ness's darkest fathoms!

Caller in the Snow

Dr. Silas Weir Mitchell retired early. A busy day at the Philadelphia hospital had worn him out. With a contented sigh he fell into bed, anticipating a good night's sleep.

Hardly had he drifted off when the doorbell rang. He struggled to hold onto sleep, hoping the caller would go away.

The doorbell rang again and again, urgently.

Dr. Mitchell sat up. There was nothing to do but throw on a robe and go downstairs.

As he descended, he looked through the living room window and saw that snow was falling on the city streets. He pulled the robe closer about him and opened the door.

Standing in the cold was a little girl. She wore a cheap, thin frock. Only a tattered shawl added protection against the snow and biting wind. She was pale and shivering.

"My mother is very sick," she said. "Won't you come, please?"

Dr Mitchell explained that he was not a general practitioner. He inquired if the girl had gone to her regular doctor — did he not live in the neighborhood?

The girl stared up at him, eyes filling with tears. She said only, "Won't you come, please?"

It was an appeal that the weary doctor had not the heart to refuse. He invited the girl inside while he put on clothes and packed a medical bag.

The girl motioned him to follow her. Wordlessly they trudged through the snowstorm to a house several blocks away. There the doctor found a woman seriously ill with pneumonia.

For a time he concentrated on treating her. When he had a moment to pause, he praised her daughter for her determination to bring him.

The woman's eyes widened in disbelief. "That cannot be," she exclaimed weakly. "My daughter died a month ago. Her clothes are in the cupboard."

Dr. Mitchell felt a chill not born of the storm. Suddenly he realized that he had not seen the little girl since he entered the house.

He opened the cupboard. Inside were the

dress and tattered shawl the girl had worn. He touched them. They were warm and dry. They could not have been out in the night storm!

That ends the story of how a ghost saved a woman's life. Did Dr. Mitchell make it up? Scarcely. He had nothing to gain and an international reputation to lose.

At the time of his death in 1914, he was America's leading neurologist and a famous man of letters. He had been president of the Association of American Physicians and of the American Neurological Association. No physician was held in higher esteem.

He related his ghost experience because, to him, it asked the question that medical science could not adequately answer: *What is death?*